chools guide to the 0 to 25 SEND code of practice

Advice for school governing bodies/proprietors, senior leadership teams, SENCOs and classroom staff

To purchase a copy please visit:

www.TheNationalCurriculum.com

or scan this code to take you there:

© Crown copyright 2014

Corporate Author: The Department For Education

Published by: Shurville Publishing

This document is available for download at www.gov.uk/government/publications

ISBN: 978-0-9930644-0-1

Contents

Foreword

Our vision for children with special educational needs and disabilities is the same as for all children – that they achieve well in their early years, at school and college, make a good transition to adulthood and lead contented and fulfilled lives.

The current system is not working for all families. The reforms introduced by the Children and Families Act 2014 aim to change this, with a focus on greater co-operation between education, health and social care and a greater focus on the outcomes which will make a real difference to how a child or young person lives their life.

Schools are vital to the success of these changes and to achieving our vision for a new system. Currently, too many children and young people do not get the support they need and support does not focus sufficiently on helping them to achieve their goals, including paid employment and independent living. With the right support and high aspirations, the vast majority of children and young people who have SEN or disabilities can achieve well and make a successful transition into adulthood, whether into employment, further or higher education or training.

Building on best practice, the 0-25 SEND Code of Practice sets clear expectations on schools to deliver a whole school approach to SEN, with good quality teaching as a first response and a clear focus on outcomes. Teachers are at the heart of the new SEN support system, supported by the strategic role of SENCOs, with strong leadership from head teachers and governors.

For the reforms to achieve a real impact, it's about long-term culture change, about having a workforce which is confident and skilled and about children and young people with SEN and disabilities having a real voice.

This guide to the Code will help you understand what your duties are under the Children and Families Act 2014 and help you navigate the full 0-25 SEND Code of Practice. It will ensure you are doing everything you should be and everything you can, to improve outcomes for this group of children and young people.

EDWARD TIMPSON

Parliamentary Under-Secretary of State
for Children and Families

About this guide

This guide is designed to help those listed below to understand their statutory duties and responsibilities under the reforms in the Children and Families Act 2014 in relation to children in their care who have or may have special educational needs or disabilities (SEND):

- Governing bodies of schools, including non-maintained special schools
- Proprietors of academies (including free schools, University Technical Colleges and Studio Schools)
- The management committees of pupil referral units
- Independent schools and independent specialist providers approved under Section 41 of the Children and Families Act 2014

In this guide 'schools' refers to all of the above, unless otherwise stated.

This guide (and the full Code of Practice) is also relevant for school leadership teams, SEN co-ordinators (SENCOs) and all classroom teachers, since it is they who will have the most day-to-day contact with pupils who have SEN or disabilities and will be responsible for delivering programmes of support for them. It is important that the entire school community understands the reforms in the 0-25 SEND Code of Practice and adopts a 'whole school' approach to supporting pupils who have SEN or disabilities.

The guide draws out elements of the full 0-25 SEND Code of Practice that relate to schools, as well as wider aspects that all those who work with children and young people with SEN or disabilities and their families should have regard to.

This document is not a substitute for the full Code of Practice and has no statutory basis. The main duties that schools must have regard to are highlighted here and links are given to the relevant sections of the Code – it is important that schools familiarise themselves with the full version of the statutory guidance in the Code in addition to reading this guide.

Expiry or review date

This guide will be kept under review and updated when necessary.

Context

The Children and Families Act 2014 provides, from September 2014, for:

- a clear and transparent 'Local Offer' of services across education, health and social care with children, young people and parents involved in preparing and reviewing it

- services across education, health and care to be jointly commissioned

- Education, Health and Care (EHC) plans to replace statements and Learning Difficulty Assessments (LDAs) with the option of a Personal Budget for families and young people who want one

- new statutory rights for young people in further education, including the right to request a particular institution is named in their EHC plan and the right to appeal to the First-tier Tribunal (SEN and Disability), and

- a stronger focus on preparing for adulthood, including better planning for transition into paid employment and independent living and between children's and adults services

From 1 September 2014 transitional arrangements will be in place to support the changeover from the current system in a phased and ordered way, to facilitate the transfer of those with statements of special educational needs to EHC plans. It is expected that all those who have a statement, and who would have continued to have one under the current system, will be transferred to an EHC plan – no-one should lose their statement and not have it replaced with an EHC plan simply because the system is changing.

A child or young person has SEN if they have a learning difficulty or disability which calls for special educational provision to be made for him or her. Children and young people who have SEN may also have a disability under the Equality Act 2010. Where a child or young person is covered by SEN and disability legislation, reasonable adjustments and access arrangements should be considered as part of SEN planning and review.

More information on the background to the SEN reforms is given in the Introduction to the 0-25 SEND Code of Practice.

Principles underlying the Code

The 0-25 SEND Code of Practice describes the principles that should be observed by all professionals working with children and young people who have SEN or disabilities. These include:

- taking into account the views of children, young people and their families
- enabling children, young people and their parents to participate in decision-making
- collaborating with partners in education, health and social care to provide support
- identifying the needs of children and young people
- making high quality provision to meet the needs of children and young people
- focusing on inclusive practices and removing barriers to learning
- helping children and young people to prepare for adulthood

More information on the principles that underpin the Children and Families Act and the guidance is given in Chapter 1, Principles, in the 0-25 SEND Code of Practice.

Working together across education, health and care for joint outcomes

Under Section 25 of the Children and Families Act 2014, local authorities have a duty to ensure integration between educational provision and training provision, health and social care provision where this would promote wellbeing and improve the quality of provision for disabled children and young people and those with SEN. This requires close co-operation with education, health and social care partners to research, plan, commission and review services.

These duties on local authorities are reciprocal – education, health and social care partners also have a duty to co-operate with the local authority on planning, commissioning and reviewing local services. For schools, this will involve contributing to the educational provision described in the local authority's Local Offer (see below), and will also involve taking part in wider strategic planning for education in the local area.

Some schools may act as commissioners of services for students with SEN or disabilities in their own right. This could include services such as speech and language therapy, pastoral care or counselling services. Joint commissioning arrangements should reflect this local commissioning and should ensure that services commissioned by schools are suitably supported to deliver positive outcomes for children and young people.

More information about joint commissioning is given in Chapter 3, Working together across education, health and care for joint outcomes, in the 0-25 SEND Code of Practice.

The Local Offer

Local authorities have a statutory duty to develop and publish a Local Offer, setting out in one place information about the support they expect to be available in their area across education, health and social care for children and young people in their area who have SEN or are disabled, including those who do not have EHC plans.

The Local Offer has two key purposes:

- To provide clear, comprehensive, accessible and up-to-date information about the available provision and how to access it, and

- To make provision more responsive to local needs and aspirations by directly involving disabled children and those with SEN and their parents, and disabled young people and those with SEN, and service providers in its development and review

Local authorities and their partner bodies and agencies, including schools, must co-operate with each other in the development and review of the Local Offer. This is essential so that the Local Offer provides a comprehensive, transparent and accessible picture of the range of services available.

The Local Offer must include, amongst other information, the following:

- special educational, health and social care provision for children and young people with SEN or disabilities – this should include online and blended learning

- other educational provision, for example sports or arts provision, paired reading schemes

- arrangements for resolving disagreements and for mediation, and details about making complaints

- arrangements for travel to and from schools

- support to help children and young people move between phases of education (for example from early years to school, from primary to secondary)

Schools will need to co-operate with the local authority to help it fulfil its duty to develop and publish in the Local Offer an authority-wide description of the special educational and training provision it expects to be available in schools in the. They should also have the opportunity to take part in the regular review of the Local Offer that the local authority has a duty to undertake, in order to identify gaps in provision and ensure that the Local Offer is responsive to the needs of local children, young people and their families.

More information about the Local Offer is available from Chapter 4, The Local Offer, in the 0-25 SEND Code of Practice.

Improving outcomes – high aspirations and expectations for children with SEN

All children and young people should expect to receive an education that enables them to achieve the best possible educational and other outcomes, and become confident, able to communicate their own views and ready to make a successful transition into adulthood, whether into employment, further or higher education or training. Underpinning this are a range of statutory duties on schools, described below.

All mainstream schools have a duty to use their best endeavours to provide support to children and young people with SEN, whether or not they have an EHC plan. They must designate a teacher to be responsible for co-ordinating SEN provision (the SEN co-ordinator or SENCO) and must inform parents when they are making special educational provision for a child.

Mainstream schools must ensure that children and young people with SEN can take part in the activities of the school alongside those who do not have SEN, and maintained schools and academies must make arrangements to support those who have medical conditions (see the statutory guidance 'Supporting pupils at school with medical conditions').

All pupils should have access to a broad and balanced curriculum. Careful planning of lessons to address potential areas of difficulty and to remove barriers to pupil achievement will mean that, in many cases, pupils with SEN and disabilities will be able to study the full curriculum.

All schools have duties under the Equality Act 2010 towards individual disabled children and young people. They must make reasonable adjustments, including the provision of auxiliary aids and services for disabled children, to prevent them being put at a substantial disadvantage. These duties are anticipatory – they require thought to be given in advance to what disabled children and young people might require and what adjustments might need to be made to prevent that disadvantage. Schools also have wider duties to prevent discrimination, to promote equality of opportunity and to foster good relations.

There should be a member of the school's governing body or a sub-committee with specific oversight of the school's arrangements for SEN and disability. School leaders should regularly review how expertise and resources used to address SEN can be used to build the quality of whole-school provision as part of their approach to school improvement.

Maintained schools and academies must prepare an SEN information report (see under SEN support in schools below) and their arrangements for the admission of disabled children, the steps being taken to prevent disabled children from being treated less favourably than others, the facilities provided to enable access to the school and their accessibility plan showing how they plan to improve access progressively over time.

Maintained schools and Pupil Referral Units (PRUs) must ensure that pupils from Year 8 until Year 13 are provided with independent careers guidance. Academies are subject to this duty through their funding agreements.

More information on these duties is given in Chapter 6, Schools, in the 0-25 SEND Code of Practice.

Identifying SEN in schools

All schools should have a clear approach to identifying and responding to SEN. The benefits of early identification are widely recognised – identifying need at the earliest point and then making effective provision improves long-term outcomes for the child or young person.

A pupil has SEN where their learning difficulty or disability calls for special educational provision, namely provision different from or additional to that normally available to pupils of the same age. Making higher quality teaching normally available to the whole class is likely to mean that fewer pupils will require such support. Such improvements in whole-class provision tend to be more cost effective and sustainable.

Under the provisions of the Children and Families Act 2014, the designations of School Action and School Action Plus have been replaced by SEN support, a graduated approach to supporting pupils with SEN or disabilities. This change will be reflected in the School Census.

Schools should assess each pupil's current skills and levels of attainment on entry, building on information from previous settings and key stages where appropriate. At the same time, schools should consider evidence that a pupil may have a disability under the Equality Act 2010 and, if so, what reasonable adjustments may need to be made for them.

Class and subject teachers, supported by the senior leadership team, should make regular assessments of progress for all pupils. These should seek to identify pupils making less than expected progress given their age and individual circumstances. This can be characterised by progress which:

- is significantly slower than that of their peers starting from the same baseline

- fails to match or better the child's previous rate of progress

- fails to close the attainment gap between the child and their peers

- widens the attainment gap

It can include progress in areas other than attainment – for instance where a pupil needs to make additional progress with wider development or social needs in order to make a successful transition to adult life.

Where a pupil is making less progress than expected, the first response to such progress should be high quality teaching targeted at their areas of weakness. Where progress continues to be less than expected the class or subject teacher, working with the SENCO, should assess whether the child has SEN. While informally gathering evidence (including the views of the pupil and their parents) schools should not delay in putting in place extra teaching or other rigorous interventions designed to secure better progress, where required. The pupil's response to such support can help identify their particular needs.

For some children, SEN can be identified at an early age. However, for other children and young people difficulties become evident only as they develop. All those who work with children and young people should be alert to emerging difficulties and respond early. In particular, parents know their children best and it is important that all professionals listen and understand when parents express concerns about their child's development. They should also listen to and address any concerns raised by children and young people themselves.

Persistent disruptive or withdrawn behaviours do not necessarily mean that a child or young person has SEN. Where there are concerns, there should be an assessment to determine whether there are any causal factors such as undiagnosed learning difficulties, difficulties with communication or mental health issues. If it is thought housing, family or other domestic circumstances may be contributing to the presenting behaviour a multi-agency approach, supported by the use of approaches such as the Early Help Assessment, may be appropriate. In all cases, early identification and intervention can significantly reduce the use of more costly intervention at a later stage.

Professionals should also be alert to other events that can lead to learning difficulties or wider mental health difficulties, such as bullying or bereavement. Such events will not always lead to children having SEN but it can have an impact on well-being and sometimes this can be severe. Schools should ensure they make appropriate provision for a child's short-term needs in order to prevent problems escalating. Where there are long-lasting difficulties schools should consider whether the child might have SEN. Further guidance on dealing with bullying issues can be found on the GOV.UK website.

Slow progress and low attainment do not necessarily mean that a child has SEN and should not automatically lead to a pupil being recorded as having SEN. However, they may be an indicator of a range of learning difficulties or disabilities. Equally, it should not be assumed that attainment in line with chronological age means that there is no learning difficulty or disability. For example, some children and young people may be high achieving academically, but may require additional support in communicating and interacting socially. Some learning difficulties and disabilities occur across the range of cognitive ability and, left unaddressed may lead to frustration, which may manifest itself as disaffection, emotional or behavioural difficulties.

Identifying and assessing SEN for children or young people whose first language is not English requires particular care. Schools should look carefully at all aspects of a child or young person's performance in different areas of learning and development or subjects to establish whether lack of progress is due to limitations in their command of English or if it arises from SEN or a disability. Difficulties related solely to limitations in English as an additional language are not SEN.

When reviewing and managing special educational provision there are four broad areas of need and support which give an overview of the range of needs that should be planned for, and schools should review how well equipped they are to provide support across these areas. They are:

- Communication and interaction
- Cognition and learning
- Social, emotion and mental health difficulties
- Sensory and/or physical needs

There is a wide range of information available on appropriate interventions for pupils with different types of need, and associated training which schools can use to ensure they have the necessary knowledge and expertise to use them. Links to organisations that provide this information are given under Useful resources at the end of this guide.

More information on identifying children and young people who have SEN and on the four broad areas of need are given in Chapter 6, Schools, in the 0-25 SEND Code of Practice (paragraphs 6.14 to 6.35).

SEN support in schools

Teachers are responsible and accountable for the progress and development of the pupils in their class, including where pupils access support from teaching assistants or specialist staff. High quality teaching, differentiated for individual pupils, is the first step in responding to pupils who have or may have SEN.

As noted in the previous section, School Action and School Action Plus have been replaced by SEN support, a graduated approach to supporting children and young people with SEN.

Deciding whether to make special educational provision

In deciding whether to make special educational provision, the teacher and SENCO should consider all of the information gathered from within the school about the pupil's progress, alongside national data and expectations of progress. This should include high quality and accurate formative assessment, using effective tools and early assessment materials. For higher levels of need, schools should have arrangements in place to draw on more specialised assessments from external agencies and professionals.

This information gathering should include an early discussion with the pupil and their parents. These early discussions with parents should be structured in such a way that they develop a good understanding of the pupil's areas of strength and difficulty, the parents' concerns, the agreed outcomes sought for the child and the next steps. A short note of these early discussions should be added to the pupil's record on the school information system and given to the parents. Schools should also tell parents and young people about the local authority's information, advice and support service.

Defining desired outcomes

Consideration of whether special educational provision is required should start with the desired outcomes, including the expected progress and attainment and the views and wishes of the pupil and their parents. This should then help determine the support that is needed and whether it can be provided by adapting the school's core offer or whether something different or additional is required.

More detailed information on what constitutes good outcome setting is given in Chapter 9, Education, Health and Care needs assessments and plans, of the 0-25 SEND Code of Practice (paragraphs 9.64 to 9.69). These principles should be applied to planning for all children and young people with SEN. From Year 9 onwards, the nature of the outcomes will reflect the need to ensure young people are preparing for adulthood.

The outcomes considered should include those needed to make successful transitions between phases of education and to prepare for adult life. Schools should engage with secondary schools or further education providers as necessary to help plan for these transitions (see Preparing for adulthood from the earliest years). The agreed actions may also include those taken to make sure the school meets its duty to ensure that pupils with SEN engage in school activities together with those who do not have SEN.

However support is provided, a clear date for reviewing progress should be agreed and the parent, pupil and teaching staff should each be clear about how they will help the pupil reach the expected outcomes. The overriding purpose of this early action is to help the pupil achieve the identified outcomes and remove any barriers to learning. Where it is decided that a pupil does have SEN, the decision should be recorded in the school records and the pupil's parents must be formally informed that special educational provision is being made. Arrangements for appropriate support should be made through the school's approach to SEN support.

SEN support – the graduated approach

Where a pupil is identified as having SEN, schools should take action to remove barriers to learning and put effective special educational provision in place. This SEN support should take the form of a four-part cycle (assess, plan, do, review) through which earlier decisions and actions are revisited, refined and revised with a growing understanding of the pupil's needs and of what supports the pupil in making good progress and securing good outcomes. This is known as the graduated approach. It draws on more detailed approaches, more frequent review and more specialist expertise in successive cycles in order to match interventions to the SEN of children and young people. More information on each stage of the graduated approach is given in Chapter 6, Schools, in the 0-25 SEND Code of Practice (paragraphs 6.45 to 6.56).

Parents should be fully aware of the planned support and interventions and, where appropriate, plans should seek parental involvement to reinforce or contribute to progress at home. Parents should also be involved in reviews of support provided to their child and have clear information about the impact of the support and interventions, enabling them to be involved in planning next steps

Planning for transition

SEN support should include planning and preparation for the transitions between phases of education and preparation for adult life (see Preparing for adulthood from the earliest years). To support transition, the school should share information with the school, college or other setting the child or young person is moving to. Schools should agree with parents and pupils the information to be shared as part of this planning process. Where a pupil is remaining at the school for post-16 provision, this planning and preparation should include consideration of how to provide a high quality study programme.

Involving specialists

Where a pupil continues to make less than expected progress, despite evidence-based support and interventions that are matched to the pupil's areas of need, the school should consider involving specialists, including those secured by the school itself or from outside agencies. This could include, for example, speech and language therapists, specialist teachers for the hearing or vision impaired, occupational therapists or physiotherapists. Schools may involve specialists at any point to advise them on early identification of SEN and effective support and interventions. The pupil's parents should always be involved in any decision to involve specialists. The involvement of specialists and what was discussed or agreed should be recorded and shared with the parents and teaching staff supporting the child in the same way as other SEN support.

The SENCO and class teacher, together with the specialists, and involving the pupil's parents, should consider a range of evidence-based and effective teaching approaches, appropriate equipment, strategies and interventions in order to support the child's progress. They should agree the outcomes to be achieved through the support, including a date by which progress will be reviewed.

Requesting an Education, Health and Care needs assessment

SEN support should be adapted or replaced depending on how effective it has been in achieving the agreed outcomes. Where, despite the school having taken relevant and purposeful action to identify, assess and meet the SEN of the child or young person, the child or young person has not made expected progress, the school or parents should consider requesting an Education, Health and Care needs assessment (see Education, health and care needs assessments and plans). To inform its decision the local authority will expect to see evidence of the action taken by the school as part of SEN support. A school may make a request for an assessment in the case of the very small minority of children and young people who may have such significant needs that the school considers it impossible or inappropriate to carry out its full chosen assessment procedure without immediate specialist assessment and interventions which it is unable to provide.

Involving parents and pupils in planning and reviewing progress

Schools **must** provide an annual report for parents on their child's progress. Most schools will want to go beyond this and provide regular reports for parents on how their child is progressing.

Where a pupil is receiving SEN support, schools should talk to parents regularly to set clear outcomes and review progress towards them, discuss the activities and support that will help achieve them, and identify the responsibilities of the parent, the pupil and the school. Schools should meet parents at least three times each year.

The views of the pupil should be included in these discussions. This could be through involving the pupil in all or part of the discussion itself, or gathering their views as part of the preparation.

A record of the outcomes, action and support agreed through the discussion should be kept and shared with all the appropriate school staff. This record should be given to the pupil's parents. The school's management information system should be updated as appropriate.

Use of data and record keeping

It is for schools to determine their own approach to record keeping in line with the requirements of the Data Protection Act 1998. The provision made for pupils with SEN should be recorded accurately and kept up to date. As part of any inspection, Ofsted will expect to see evidence of pupil progress, a focus on outcomes and a rigorous approach to the monitoring and evaluation of any SEN support provided. Ofsted publish more detail about their expectations in their inspection guidelines. More information on record keeping and provision management is given in Chapter 6, Schools, in the 0-25 SEND Code of Practice (paragraphs 6.72 to 6.78).

SEN information report

The governing bodies of maintained schools and maintained nursery schools and the proprietors of academy schools must publish information on their websites about the implementation of the governing body's or the proprietor's policy for pupils with SEN. This information can be included as part of the school's overall SEN policy and does not need to be a separate document. The information published should be updated annually and any changes to the information occurring during the year should be updated as soon as possible. Details of the information required are given in Chapter 6, Schools, in the 0-25 SEND Code of Practice (paragraph 6.79).

Schools should ensure that the information is easily accessible by young people and parents and is set out in clear, straightforward language. It should include information on the school's SEN policy and named contacts within the school for situations where young people or parents have concerns. It should also give details of the school's contribution to the Local Offer and must include information on where the local authority's Local Offer is published.

In setting out details of the broad and balanced curriculum provided in each year, schools should include details of how the curriculum is adapted or made accessible for pupils with SEN.

Schools should also make any data it collects on the levels and types of need within the school available to the local authority. This data will be required to inform local strategic planning of SEN support, and to enable the local authority to identify pupils who have or may have SEN. Such data, as collected through the School Census, is also required to produce the national SEN information report.

Role of the SENCO

Governing bodies of maintained mainstream schools and the proprietors of mainstream academy schools (including free schools) must ensure that there is a qualified teacher designated as SENCO for the school.

The SENCO must be a qualified teacher working at the school. A newly appointed SENCO must be a qualified teacher and, where they have not previously been the SENCO at that or any other relevant school for a total period of more than twelve months, they must achieve a National Award in Special Educational Needs Co-ordination within three years of appointment.

A National Award must be a postgraduate course accredited by a recognised higher education provider. The National College for Teaching and Leadership has worked with providers to develop a set of learning outcomes (see the References section under Chapter 6 for a link). When appointing staff or arranging for them to study for a National Award schools should satisfy themselves that the chosen course will meet these outcomes and equip the SENCO to fulfil the duties outlined in this Code. Any selected course should be at least equivalent to 60 credits at postgraduate study.

The SENCO has an important role to play with the headteacher and governing body, in determining the strategic development of SEN policy and provision in the school. They will be most effective in that role if they are part of the school leadership team.

The SENCO has day-to-day responsibility for the operation of SEN policy and co-ordination of specific provision made to support individual pupils with SEN, including those who have EHC plans. The key duties of the SENCO are outlined in Chapter 6, Schools, in the 0-25 SEND Code of Practice (paragraph 6.90).

The SENCO provides professional guidance to colleagues and will work closely with staff, parents and other agencies. The SENCO should be aware of the provision in the Local Offer and be able to work with professionals providing a support role to families to ensure that pupils with SEN receive appropriate support and high quality teaching.

The school should ensure that the SENCO has sufficient time and resources to carry out these functions. This should include providing the SENCO with sufficient administrative support and time away from teaching to enable them to fulfil their responsibilities in a similar way to other important strategic roles within a school.

It may be appropriate for a number of smaller primary schools to share a SENCO employed to work across the individual schools, where they meet the other requirements set out in this chapter of the Code. Schools can consider this arrangement where it secures sufficient time away from teaching and sufficient administrative support to enable the SENCO to fulfil the role effectively for the total registered pupil population across all of the schools involved.

Where such a shared approach is taken the SENCO should not normally have a significant class teaching commitment. Such a shared SENCO role should not be carried out by a headteacher at one of the schools.

Schools should review the effectiveness of such a shared SENCO role regularly and should not persist with it where there is evidence of a negative impact on the quality of SEN provision, or the progress of pupils with SEN.

Funding for SEN support

All mainstream schools are provided with resources to support those with additional needs, including pupils with SEN and disabilities. Most of these resources are determined by a local funding formula, discussed with the local schools forum, which is also applied to local academies. School and academy sixth forms receive an allocation based on a national funding formula.

Schools have an amount identified within their overall budget, called the notional SEN budget. This is not a ring-fenced amount, and it is for the school to provide high quality appropriate support from the whole of its budget.

It is for schools, as part of their normal budget planning, to determine their approach to using their resources to support the progress of pupils with SEN. The SENCO, headteacher and governing body or proprietor should establish a clear picture of the resources that are available to the school. They should consider their strategic approach to meeting SEN in the context of the total resources available, including any resources targeted at particular groups, such as the pupil premium.

This will enable schools to provide a clear description of the types of special educational provision they normally provide and will help parents and others to understand what they can normally expect the school to provide for pupils with SEN.

Schools are not expected to meet the full costs of more expensive special educational provision from their core funding. They are expected to provide additional support which costs up to a nationally prescribed threshold per pupil per year. The responsible local authority, usually the authority where the child or young person lives, should provide additional top-up funding where the cost of the special educational provision required to meet the needs of an individual pupil exceeds the nationally prescribed threshold.

More information on schools' duties and responsibilities in relation to children and young people with SEN or disabilities is given in Chapter 6, Schools, in the 0-25 SEND Code of Practice.

Preparing for adulthood from the earliest years

Everyone working with children and young people who have SEN or disabilities should support them to prepare for adult life and help them go on to achieve the best outcomes in employment, independent living, health and community participation.

Starting early

When a child is very young, or SEN is first identified, families need to know that the great majority of children and young people with SEN or disabilities, with the right support, can find work, be supported to live independently, and participate in their community. Health workers, social workers, early years providers and schools should encourage these ambitions right from the start. They should seek to understand the interests, strengths and motivations of children and young people and use this as a basis for planning support around them.

Schools should support children and young people so that they are included in social groups and develop friendships. This is particularly important when children and young people are transferring from one phase of education to another (for example, from nursery to primary school). Maintained schools must ensure that, subject to certain conditions, pupils with SEN engage in the activities of the school together with those who do not have SEN, and are encouraged to participate fully in the life of the school and in any wider community activity.

Support from Year 9 onwards (age 13-14)

High aspirations about employment, independent living and community participation should be developed through the curriculum and extra-curricular provision. Schools should seek partnerships with employment services, businesses, housing agencies, disability organisations and arts and sports groups, to help children understand what is available to them as they get older, and what it is possible for them to achieve. It can be particularly powerful to meet disabled adults who are successful in their work or who have made a significant contribution to their community.

Preparing for adulthood reviews

Preparing for adulthood should form part of the planning for all children and young people with SEN and disabilities, right from the earliest years. However, for teenagers preparation for adult life needs to be a more explicit element of their planning and support. Discussions about their future should focus on what they want to achieve and the best way to support them to achieve. For children and young people with EHC plans, local authorities must ensure that the EHC plan review at Year 9, and every review thereafter, includes a focus on preparing for adulthood. Information about what should be included in preparing for adulthood reviews is given in Chapter 8, Preparing for adulthood from the earliest years, in the 0-25 SEND Code of Practice (paragraphs 8.11 to 8.14).

Young people's right to make their own decisions

After compulsory school age (the end of the academic year in which they turn 16) the right to make requests and decisions under the Children and Families Act 2014 applies to young people directly, rather than to their parents. Parents, or other family members, can continue to support young people in making decisions, or act on their behalf, provided that the young person is happy for them to do so, and it is likely that parents will remain closely involved in the great majority of cases.

This is particularly important for young people under 18 and schools would normally involve parents or family members where they have concerns about a young person's behaviour or welfare. They should also continue to involve parents or family members in discussions about the young person's studies where that is their usual policy. The fact that the Children and Families Act 2014 gives rights directly to young people from the end of compulsory school age does not necessitate any change to a school's safeguarding or welfare policy.

Planning the transition into post-16 education and training

Young people entering post-16 education and training should be accessing provision which supports them to build on their achievements at school and which helps them progress towards adulthood. Young people with EHC plans are likely to need more tailored post-16 pathways.

It is important that information about previous SEN provision is shared with the further education or training provider. Schools should share information before the young person takes up their place, preferably in the spring term prior to the new course, so that the provider can develop a suitable study programme and prepare appropriate support.

Schools and colleges should work in partnership to provide opportunities such as taster courses, link programmes and mentoring which enable young people with SEN to familiarise themselves with the college environment and gain some experience of college life and study.

For children and young people with EHC plans, discussions about post-16 options will be part of the preparing for adulthood focus of EHC plan reviews, which must be included as part of the review from Year 9 (age 13-14). The local authority must ensure these reviews take place, and schools must co-operate with the local authority in these reviews. If it is clear that a young person wants to attend a different school (sixth form) or a college, then that school or college must co-operate, so that it can help to shape the EHC plan, help to define the outcomes for that young person and start developing a post-16 study programme tailored to their needs.

Careers advice for children and young people

Maintained schools and pupil referral units (PRUs) have a statutory duty under section 42A of the Education Act 1997 to ensure pupils from Year 8 until Year 13 are provided with independent careers guidance. Academies, including 16-19 academies, and free schools are subject to this duty through their Funding Agreements.

Schools should raise the career aspirations of students with SEN and broaden their employment horizons. They should use a wide range of imaginative approaches, such as taster opportunities, work experience, mentoring, exploring entrepreneurial options, role models and inspiring speakers.

High quality study programmes for pupils with SEN

All pupils aged 16-19 should follow a coherent study programme which provides stretch and progression and enables them to achieve the best possible outcomes in adult life. Schools are expected to design study programmes which enable pupils to progress to a higher level of study than their prior attainment, take rigorous, substantial qualifications, study English and maths, participate in meaningful work experience and non-qualification activity. They should not be repeating learning they have already completed successfully. For pupils who are not taking qualifications, their study programme should focus on high quality work experience, and on non-qualification activity which prepares them well for employment, independent living, being healthy adults and participating in society. Full guidance about study programmes is available on the GOV.UK website.

Pathways to employment

All young people should be helped to develop the skills and experience, and achieve the qualifications they need, to succeed in their careers. The vast majority of young people with SEN are capable of sustainable paid employment with the right preparation and support. All professionals working with them should share that presumption. One of the most effective ways to prepare young people with SEN for employment is to arrange work-based learning that enables them to have first-hand experience of work, such as apprenticeships, traineeships and supported internships. More information about pathways to employment for children and young people who have SEN or disabilities is given in Chapter 8, Preparing for adulthood from the earliest years, in the 0-25 SEND Code of Practice (paragraphs 8.33 to 8.40).

Transition to higher education

Securing a place in higher education is a positive outcome for many young people with SEN or a disability. Where a young person has this ambition, the right level of provision and support should be provided to help them to achieve that goal, wherever possible.

Leaving education or training

All young people with SEN should be supported to make the transition to life beyond school or college, whether or not they have an EHC plan. As well as preparing them for adulthood generally, schools should ensure that young people with SEN have the information they need to make the final steps in this transition. This includes information about local employers, further training, and where to go for further advice or support.

For young people with EHC plans, where it is known that a young person will soon be completing their time in education and training, the annual review prior to ceasing the EHC plan should be used to agree the support and specific steps needed to help the young person to engage with the services and provision they will be accessing once they have left education, and the school should contribute to this review.

More information about helping young people to prepare for adulthood is in Chapter 8, Preparing for adulthood from the earliest years, in the 0-25 SEND Code of Practice.

Education, health and care needs assessments and plans

Schools must co-operate with local authorities in carrying out needs assessments for pupils, and in the development and review of EHC plans. They also have a duty to admit a young person to the school if it is named in their EHC plan and to provide the educational support specified in the plan.

EHC needs assessments

Where, despite the school having taken relevant and purposeful action to identify, assess and meet the SEN of a child or young person, the child or young person has not made expected progress, the school or the child's parents could consider asking the local authority to carry out an Education, Health and Care (EHC) needs assessment.

During the course of an EHC needs assessment, the local authority must gather advice from relevant professionals about the young person's education, health and care needs, desired outcomes and special educational, health and care provision that may be required to meet the identified needs and achieve desired outcomes. The school should co-operate with the local authority in this, by providing the educational advice and information requested.

Being named in an EHC plan

The child's parent or the young person has the right to request a particular school to be named in their EHC plan. This can be a maintained school, any form of academy or free school (mainstream or special), a non-maintained special school, or an independent school or independent special school (where they have been approved by the Secretary of State for this purpose under Section 41 of the Children and Families Act 2014). The local authority must consult the governing body of that school about admitting the child or young person and to name the school in the EHC plan, unless:

- it would be unsuitable for the age, ability, aptitude or SEN of the child or young person, or

- the attendance of the child or young person there would be incompatible with the efficient education of others or the efficient use of resources

The local authority must consider the comments of the school carefully before deciding to name it in an EHC plan. Once the school is named in the EHC plan, it must admit the child or young person.

The child's parent or the young person may also make representations for a place at an independent school that is not on the list of schools approved by the Secretary of State under Section 41 of the Children and Families Act 2014 and the local authority must consider their request. The local authority is not under the same conditional duty to name the school but must have regard to the general principle in section 9 of the Education Act 1996 that children should be educated in accordance with their parents' wishes, so long as this is compatible with the provision of efficient instruction and training and does not mean unreasonable public expenditure. The local authority should be satisfied that the school would admit the child or young person before naming it in a plan since these providers are not subject to the duty to admit a child or young person even if named in their plan.

Providing the support specified in the EHC plan

Section F of the EHC plan specifies the special educational provision required by the young person in order to ensure it meets their needs and will help them to achieve their desired outcomes. The local authority must make sure this support is provided. The school will have been involved in the development or review of the EHC plan to determine what can be provided from within the school's own resources and what will require additional external expertise or further funding from the local authority.

Some of the provision specified may be procured by the child's parent or the young person using a Personal Budget, including by a direct payment. Where a direct payment is to be used to deliver provision on the school premises, the local authority must seek the agreement of the school for this arrangement through a formal written notice.

Reviewing an EHC plan

Local authorities have a duty to review EHC plans as a minimum every twelve months, and schools must co-operate in these reviews. Reviews must focus on the child or young person's progress towards achieving the outcomes specified in the EHC plan and must also consider whether these outcomes and supporting targets remain appropriate.

Reviews of EHC plans must include a focus on preparing for adulthood and transition planning must be built into the plan. In particular, where a young person is nearing the end of their time in formal education and the plan is likely to be ceased within the next 12 months, the annual review should consider good exit planning.

The local authority can require a maintained school, non-maintained special school, academy, alternative provision academy, PRU school or independent school approved by the Secretary of State under Section 41 of the Children and Families Act 2014 to convene and hold the review meeting on their behalf. In most cases, reviews should normally be held at the educational institution attended by the child or young person. Reviews are generally most effective when led by the educational institution. They know the child or young person best, will have the closest contact with them and their family and will have the clearest information about progress and next steps. Reviews led by the educational institution will engender the greatest confidence amongst the child, young person and their family.

The child's parents or the young person, a representative of the school or other institution attended, a local authority SEN officer, a health service representative and a local authority social care representative must be invited and given at least two weeks' notice of the date of the meeting. Other individuals relevant to the review should also be invited, including youth offending teams and job coaches where relevant.

The school must seek advice and information about the child or young person prior to the meeting from all parties invited, and send any advice and information gathered to all those invited at least two weeks before the meeting.

The meeting must focus on the child or young person's progress towards achieving the outcomes specified in the EHC plan, and on what changes might need to be made to the support that is provided to help them achieve those outcomes, or whether changes are needed to the outcomes themselves. Children, parents and young people should be supported to engage fully in the review meeting.

The school must prepare and send a report of the meeting to everyone invited within two weeks of the meeting. The report must set out recommendations on any amendments required to the EHC plan, and should refer to any difference between the school or other institution's recommendations and those of others attending the meeting.

Transfer between phases of education

An EHC plan must be reviewed and amended in sufficient time prior to a child or young person moving between key phases of education, to allow for planning for and, where necessary, commissioning of support and provision at the new institution.

The review and any amendments must be completed by 15 February in the calendar year of the transfer at the latest for transfers into or between schools. The key transfers are:

- early years provider to school
- infant school to junior school
- primary school to middle school
- primary school to secondary school, and
- middle school to secondary school

For young people moving from secondary school to a post-16 institution or apprenticeship, the review and any amendments to the EHC plan – including specifying the post-16 provision and naming the institution – must be completed by the 31 March in the calendar year of the transfer.

Preparing for adulthood reviews

All reviews taking place from year 9 at the latest and onwards must include a focus on preparing for adulthood, including employment, independent living and participation in society. This transition planning must be built into the EHC plan and where relevant should include effective planning for young people moving from children's to adult care and health services. It is particularly important in these reviews to seek and to record the views, wishes and feelings of the child or young person. The review meeting organiser should invite representatives of post-16 institutions to these review meetings, particularly where the child or young person has expressed a desire to attend a particular institution. Review meetings taking place in year 9 should have a particular focus on considering options and choices for the next phase of education.

As the young person is nearing the end of their time in formal education and the plan is likely to be ceased within the next 12 months, the annual review should consider good exit planning. Support, provision and outcomes should be agreed that will ensure the young person is supported to make a smooth transition to whatever they will be doing next – for example, moving on to higher education, employment, independent living or adult care.

More information on EHC plans is given in Chapter 9, Education, Health and Care needs assessments and plans, in the 0-25 SEND Code of Practice.

Children and young people in specific circumstances

There are particular groups of children and young people whose specific circumstances require additional consideration by those who work with them and support their SEN, including schools.

Looked after children

Children who are being accommodated, or who have been taken into care, by a local authority are legally defined as being 'looked after' by the local authority. Around 70% of looked after children have some form of SEN, and it is likely that a significant proportion of them will have an EHC plan.

All maintained schools and academies and free schools must appoint a Designated Teacher for looked after children. Where that role is carried out by a person other than the SEN Co-ordinator (SENCO), Designated Teachers should work closely with the SENCO to ensure that the implications of a child being both looked after and having SEN are fully understood by relevant school staff.

Local authorities must promote the educational achievement of the children they look after, regardless of where they are placed. The Children and Families Act 2014 requires every local authority to appoint an officer who is an employee of that or another authority to discharge that duty. This officer, often known as a Virtual School Head (VSH) will lead a virtual school team, which tracks the progress of children looked after by the authority as if they attended a single school.

Children and young people with SEN educated at home

Under section 7 of the Education Act 1996 parents have the right to educate children, including children with SEN, at home. Where a child or young person is a registered pupil and the parent decides to home educate, the parent must notify the school in writing that the child or young person is receiving education otherwise than at school and the school must then remove the pupil's name from the admission register. If the school is a special school, the local authority must give consent for the child's name to be removed, but this should not be a lengthy or complex process. There is no provision in law for a 'trial period' of home education.

Children with SEN who are in alternative provision

Local authorities must make arrangements where, for any reason, a child of compulsory school age would not otherwise receive suitable education. Suitable education means efficient education suitable to a child or young person's age, ability and aptitude and to any SEN he or she may have. This education must be full-time, unless the local authority determines that, for reasons relating to the physical or mental health of the child, a reduced level of education would be in the child's best interests.

Where this education is arranged elsewhere than at a school it is commonly referred to as alternative provision. Alternative provision includes pupil referral units, alternative provision academies and alternative provision free schools. Schools may commission alternative provision for children and young people who face barriers to participation in mainstream education or training. Alternative provision must be arranged in line with a child or young person's EHC plan. Where a child or young person in alternative provision has SEN that are not specified in an EHC plan then the alternative provider should employ a graduated response to these needs (see the section on SEN support in schools in this guide).

Children of Service personnel

The Children's Education Advisory Service (CEAS) within the Ministry of Defence provides advice and guidance to Service parents, educational establishments and local authorities on educational issues relating to Service children, including issues relating to SEN.

Children whose parent(s) are Service personnel may face difficulties that are unique to the nature of their serving parent's employment. These needs may arise from:

- **service-induced mobility:** Service personnel may relocate more often than the rest of the population and, sometimes, at short notice. Such transitions should be well managed to avoid Service children with SEN experiencing delays in having their needs assessed and met

- the **deployment** of serving parents to operational arenas, while not constituting SEN in itself, may result in a Service child experiencing anxiety, dips in educational performance and/or emotional difficulties. Children may also be affected similarly by siblings' deployment

In having regard to this Code of Practice and in meeting the aspirations of the Armed Forces Covenant, which attempts to eliminate or mitigate some of the potential disadvantages faced by Service families, all those with statutory responsibilities towards Service children with SEN should ensure that the impact of their policies, administrative processes and patterns of provision do not disadvantage such children because of their Service-related lifestyle.

In respect of Service children, schools and other education providers should:

- ensure that mechanisms are in place to enable effective and timely receipt and dispatch of all relevant records for Service children with SEN moving between schools in the UK and overseas, to enable effective planning, ideally in advance of the child's arrival in school. Maintained schools must transfer information, including SEN information, about pupils to other schools in the UK (maintained or independent) in accordance with the Education (Pupil Information)

Regulations 2005. To support the transfer of information on Service children with SEN the MoD has developed the Pupil Information Profile for Service children, which includes details of a child's SEN. It is available for use by schools across the UK and overseas and is available from the Children's Education Advisory Service (CEAS) on the GOV.UK website

- ensure that all reviews for Service children with SEN explicitly consider those Service-related issues (for example, Service-induced mobility) relevant to the outcomes of those reviews

- ensure that access to appropriate assessments, interventions and provision is determined solely on the nature, severity and complexity of the needs presented by Service children with SEN and not related to the amount of time they have left in a particular school

- consider how any funds received through the Service Pupils' Premium might be used to improve their overall approaches to meeting the SEN of Service children

More information on children whose specific circumstances may affect their SEN or disability is available from Chapter 10, Children and young people in specific circumstances, in the 0-25 SEND Code of Practice.

Resolving disagreements

All state-funded schools are required to have a procedure to deal with complaints and to publish details of their procedure. This does not include complaints relating to EHC plans, which pupils and their families should take up with the local authority that issued the plan.

The governing bodies of maintained schools should make efforts to ensure that anyone who wishes to make a complaint, including a complaint in relation to children and young people with SEN, whether they have EHC plans or not, is treated fairly, given the chance to state their case, provided with a written response (including the rationale for any decisions) and informed of their appeal rights. If the complainant remains concerned after following the local complaints procedure, he or she could ask the Department for Education's School Complaints Unit to take up the matter.

Further details on making complaints to the Department about schools are available from the GOV.UK website.

The proprietors of academies, free schools and independent schools must, under the Education (Independent School Standards) Regulations 2010, ensure that a complaints procedure is drawn up which is in writing and is made available to parents. The procedure must allow for a complaint to be considered informally in the first instance and then, if the parent remains dissatisfied, there should be a formal procedure for the complaint to be made in writing. If the parent is still dissatisfied the complaint can then be heard in front of a panel of at least three people one of whom must be independent of the management and running of the school. Should the parent still not be satisfied they can complain, in the case of academies and free schools, to the Education Funding Agency (EFA) acting on behalf of the Secretary of State, or, in the case of independent schools, to the Secretary of State directly. Both the EFA and the Secretary of State will look at whether the school handled the complaint properly, rather than the substance of the complaint. Further details on making a complaint to the EFA about academies and free schools are also available at the weblink given in the previous paragraph.

Schools complaints procedures are available for use in relation to children and young people who have SEN, but do not have EHC plans.

Further information about complaints is given in Chapter 11, Resolving disagreements, in the 0-25 SEND Code of Practice.

Useful resources

Legislation and statutory guidance

0-25 Special Educational Needs and Disability Code of Practice

Children and Families Act 2014

Education Act 1996

Equality Act 2010

Special Educational Needs (Personal Budgets) Regulations 2014

Special Educational Needs and Disability Regulations 2014

Other Government information

Bullying guidance

Education Funding Agency (EFA)

First-tier Tribunal (Special Educational Needs and Disability)

Mental Health and Behaviour in Schools Guidance

National Award for SENCO Co-ordination: learning outcomes

Participation of young people in education, employment and training (DfE guidance)

Pathfinder information packs

Preparing for Adulthood

Provision mapping resources

Reasonable adjustments for disabled pupils 2012

Social Care for Deafblind Children and Adults guidance 2009 (DoH)

Supporting pupils at school with medical conditions

Working Together to Safeguard Children 2013

Best practice examples/websites

Achievement for All

Autism Education Trust

Communication Trust

Council for Disabled Children

Dyslexia SpLD Trust

I CAN – the children's communications charity

MindEd

nasen

National Sensory Impairment Partnership

SEND Gateway